Life's simple recipes

Bringing Tired and Busy Women Back to Balance

Denice Cartwright
pure peace

THOUGHTFUL RAVEN
LONDON, ENGLAND

Copyright © 2024 Denice Cartwright
All rights reserved.

For permissions or enquiries contact:
denice@purepeace.co.uk

A THOUGHTFUL RAVEN Book
www.thoughtfulraven.co.uk

ISBN: 9798342654999

Readers are encouraged to use their own discretion and judgement when applying any recipes or suggestions provided in this book. The content of this book is based on personal experiences, opinions and research and is not intended to replace professional advice and support. If you are experiencing emotional distress, mental health challenges or medical conditions, please seek appropriate support from a qualified professional.

Life's Simple Recipes
First Edition, November 2024

Welcome

Before you begin browsing and pondering the recipes within the safe space of this book, let me introduce myself to you through this short video.

Or you'll find the welcome video and a hand-picked selection of free resources at:

https://bit.ly/tr_tired_busy_women

The warmest of welcomes to some time with YOU.

Denice x

I dedicate this book to them women who often feel a disconnect from life. Those who don't naturally make time to do the things they love. Those who often feel tired and out of balance.

I dedicate this book to you because recognising this disconnect is the first step to being more loving towards yourself. Each step you take creates a more balanced and peaceful world - and for that I thank you.

*"Never have I craved a love so deeply
as the love of myself"*

Herman Melville 1819-1891

Contents

PART ONE 1
   DEHYDRATION.. 7
   SLEEP & REST 19
   MESS & CLUTTER 31
   SLOWING DOWN TO GET MORE DONE............... 41
   SELF-SABOTAGE.................................... 53
   JUDGEMENT 65
   RESENTMENT 77
   COMMITMENT 87

PART TWO 99
   NERVOUS SYSTEM CALLING 103
   MORE BALANCE IN WHAT YOU LOVE 115
   SAFETY 129
   KINDNESS AS A VALUE..................................... 139
   CLUTTERED THINKING, BELIEFS AND HABITS.... 153
   LONELINESS....................................... 165
   BEING COMFORTABLE WITH QUIETNESS 177
   UNPLUGGING...................................... 187
   BEING UNCONTACTABLE................................. 197

CLOSING THOUGHTS.............................. 207

Foreword

Denice has written this book KNOWING that her recipes deliver beautiful results, because they are all born of walking her own talk.

This is the kind of book you can pick up and read once, or read it ten times, and you will get inspiration from it each and every time.

Whether it's one page, one recipe, or the whole book, you will find nuggets of wisdom and heaps of ideas that will make you think about your life – and more importantly, think about yourself.

Life's Simple Recipes is about introducing small, sensible, practical changes to then bring about much bigger change, rather than making dramatic all-encompassing changes, which often creates feelings of overwhelm and inertia.

A key point Denice makes is about creating space for stillness - even for just 30 seconds.

Modern life can be noisy and crowded from the second you wake up, to the moment you go to bed, and then you wonder why you can't get to sleep.

Denice gently guides you to a place of stillness and silence and supports you to be more comfortable in this space.

For every woman, of every age, I invite you to share these recipes with other women you know. Teach your young ones the simple act of stopping, alongside the importance of stillness and the value of building a true relationship with yourself.

First and foremost, practice the recipes for yourself and notice the difference they start to make in your life.

FOREWORD

I've known Denice for 18 years. We have walked a path of personal healing, well-being and exploring the bigger picture of life together, and I know she comes from a place of deep truth in writing this book.

Her words are not empty words - they are words she lives herself, full of wisdom, full of love, and full of knowing that the ingredients, steps, principles and tools she offers you really do help, and really do make a difference.

Life's Simple Recipes for Bringing Tired and Busy Women Back to Balance will change your life.

Shelley Sishton. Author and Story Weaver,
Flower Medicine Teacher, Film Producer.
www.shelleysishton.com

Dear Reader

If you've picked this book up, the chances are that you know what being exhausted and a little lost from yourself can feel like. Or maybe you know someone who lives those cycles often and you are reading it for them.

Whichever is the case, I want to welcome you to this time with yourself. I acknowledge you for making this decision, in what already feels like a busy and sometimes cluttered life.

My motivation for writing this book is to name and spend time with the foundations of balance, which I consider essential if we want to live a life of true happiness.

This book speaks to women who rarely put their attention into the needs of their own lives, because they are tired and often overwhelmed in supporting others.

LIFE'S SIMPLE RECIPES

This is for women who wear many masks of roles, such as: mother, wife, daughter, friend, colleague, sister or confidant. Those who live their lives from those roles, barely expressing the person hidden inside.

This book of simple recipes has your back, has your heart and I hope has some of your precious time.

I have used the analogy of keeping your kitchen clean to represent your life. I wanted to keep it light, practical and for it to be a book of ease and common sense.

A clean and tidy kitchen makes the art of cooking so much easier and more enjoyable, after all. The same goes for everyday living.

After that, Part Two is designed to take you deeper into your often untouched inner world. We are going to see what beliefs, emotions and conditions are running unconscious patterns in the background of your life.

Going deeper will support you to explore the signals your mind and body offers to you as feedback and support you to advocate with ease, due to more awareness of your own needs. It will invite you to spend more time getting to know yourself. These are vital ingredients for a balanced and energised life and are shared in a way which I hope you find comfortable and interesting.

I hope you feel refreshed in the simplicity of the suggestions in these recipes. Maybe they seem obvious, but they are guaranteed to make a BIG difference in how you experience your own knowing of balance and happiness.

Read this book your way, from start to finish, or picking what speaks to you. Either way, dive in!

Much love,
Denice x

PART ONE

A look at the foundations to living
a more balanced life

LIFE'S SIMPLE RECIPES

Cleaning Your Kitchen

What does that even mean?

It's an analogy I've created to simplify this understanding: You can't prepare, make, enjoy and share your beautiful bakes and nutrition with those in your life if your kitchen is in an overwhelm of chaos, mess, lack of space and confusion in knowing where or how to find a starting point.

In the same way, it's difficult to create a life of balance and to share your fullest self with the world, if your life is often in overwhelm. Chaos, mess, lack of space and confusion are overwhelming. It can be hard to know where or how to find a starting point.

Maslow's Hierarchy of Needs diagram (1943), which can be seen in appendix at the back of this book, suggests that if we want to live to our full potential, meeting our basic needs is essential.

Although these needs are not linear or a prescriptive order of requirement, not tending to them will influence how life feels for you.

So, cleaning your kitchen is about two things:

First some focused inner reflection, a noticing of what soothes your nervous system, what triggers it into stress.

And then an honest inventory on what changes or tiny tweaks you could make, to alter your body's capacity to manage stress.

Cleaning your kitchen starts with soothing your nervous system as this is the foundation from which your life unfolds.

If you're committed to regularly cleaning your kitchen as a dedication to supporting your nervous system, life will have more solid roots. And these roots help us stay more grounded, as and when turbulence arrives.

PART ONE: CLEANING YOUR KITCHEN

How can you do this?

You start with the basics. I'm sharing recipes to help you clean your kitchen. Some recipes suggest actions whilst others offer a space for reflection. Both will support you with this clean-up of your metaphorical kitchen.

There is space for jotting down any notes at the end of each chapter...Very helpful if you easily forget changes you decide you would like to try.

Let's get started...

No one needs advising or showing how to clean a kitchen up. It's pretty obvious, yet it's something which continues to not get the due attention it deserves, especially when feeling tired and busy.

It would be easy for me to leave Part One unspoken, to not touch the uncomfortableness of saying the obvious, but that would do what's to follow in Part Two a total disservice.

To ignore the obvious and to not check in with it will have our balance interrupted when life speeds up.

So, let's get on with the most obvious, so that it holds us in place for when life feels busy.

What are the obvious points we're talking about here?

- Dehydration
- Sleep & rest
- Mess & clutter
- Slowing down to get more done
- Self-sabotage
- Self-judgement
- Resentment
- Commitment

♡

DEHYDRATION

Brain fog, procrastination, judgement, anxiety and frustrations.

Triggered, tired and a block to feeling vibrancy.

Have you ever considered that these sensations are intensified when we aren't hydrated?

You may well be surprised with the difference a pint of water makes to your sense of energy and wellbeing.

Incredibly simple BUT not to be overlooked...

Hydration is a fundamental pillar of feeling balanced, yet one so often forgotten and underestimated.

Water is your body's principal chemical component and makes up about 50% to 70% of your body weight. Your body depends on water to survive.

Every cell, tissue and organ in your body needs water to work properly. Water lubricates joints, regulates our temperature and gets rid of wastes through urination, perspiration and bowel movements.

Hydration is vital for being in balance and so seems an obvious place to start when we feel out of sorts and off our usual balance.

♡

DEHYDRATION

Possible indicators and symptoms of dehydration (amongst many more)

Brain fog, joint pain, anxiety, procrastination, irritation, indecisiveness, headaches, hunger, tiredness, thirst, sunken eyes and dry skin.

LIFE'S SIMPLE RECIPES

RECIPES FOR DEHYDRATION

Recipe 1 – Cellular Hydrating Linseed Tea

Recipe 2 – Staying Hydrated

Recipe 3 – Put Hydration to the Test

Recipe 4 – Making Hydration Easier

Recipe 5 – Hydration Reminders

Recipe 1 – Cellular Hydrating Linseed Tea

Ingredients:

1 tbsp of whole linseeds

1 litre of filtered water

Optional cinnamon stick, cloves or star anise.

Instructions:

1. Put linseeds in a saucepan with the filtered water and soak over night
2. Add any optional spices, bring to the boil in the soaked water and simmer for 10 mins. If the tea is too thick for you, add some extra water
3. Strain and discard the linseeds and enjoy your tea

Recipe 2 – Staying Hydrated

How much water should I be drinking?

A simple suggestion here, as we are all different and it can depend on what dehydrating foods you are consuming or the temperature of the environment you are within. It doesn't come simpler than this.

Check the colour of your urine? That's it...If it's not light yellow or close to pale in colour then you need to be drinking more water.

Recipe 3 – Put Hydration to the Test

To find out if hydration really helps you to feel more emotionally stable, why not log it?

If you notice you are feeling a little stressed or overwhelmed in your thinking, log or notice how you are feeling, have a pint of water and notice how you are feeling an hour later. Tuning in and noticing for yourself is the feedback and inspiration for knowing if this is a truth for you or not.

Recipe 4 – Making Hydration Easier

It can be as simple as this...

Purchasing a nice new water bottle can be a great encourager and reminder to increase your water intake. Women I've spoken to who struggle to drink water have said that a bottle with a straw makes it easier for them. They say that the use of the straw makes it easier to swallow and before they know it, their bottle is empty. So, if you struggle, a bottle with a straw may be a good idea and work for you.

Recipe 5 – Hydration Reminders

Purchasing or using a water jug, which you fill in the morning and leave on your kitchen side or desk will be a brilliant reminder. Maybe add some lemons, limes or blueberries, which will have an alkalising effect on your body. Having these reminders, if drinking water isn't a normal habit for you, can be helpful.

DEHYDRATION

For Your Notes...

SLEEP & REST

Emotional, knot in stomach, apathy, mood swings and impatience.

Lack of motivation, distraction, tearfulness and anger.

Feeling a little sorry for oneself, accident prone, anxious and dazed.

Head hits the pillow, and your mind awakens, over tired, annoyed and the cycle starts again, with an almost dread or avoidance of a bedtime routine.

An obvious subject, but one to look at if you find that sleep can be an issue for you. Lack of sleep will have a massive effect on how you feel and function in your life...of course it will!

It can be an upsetting subject for people who have issues with sleep and so it's worth the time to explore how your sleep pattern looks. To explore what supports it, what creates issues and what you can do to help yourself make it the best quality that's possible at this time.

♡

SLEEP & REST

Possible indicators and symptoms of lack of sleep and/or rest (amongst many more)

Headaches, muscle weakness, slower reflexes/responses, lack of energy, impaired decision-making, moodiness, upset emotions, emotional eating, mild depression, anxiousness and near misses or actual accidents.

LIFE'S SIMPLE RECIPES

RECIPES FOR SLEEP & REST

Recipe 1 – Sleeping Environment

Recipe 2 – Clearing the Mind

Recipe 3 – Sleep Routines

Recipe 4 – Move Towards Tired

Recipe 5 – Conscious Resting

Recipe 1 – Sleeping Environment

A calm and clear sleeping space makes such a difference to sleep. You may not notice it at first, but it will deepen the quality of your sleep if your room and sleeping area is clear of clutter. Your body will relax more easily when there is more space and less clutter to look at, be around and within the energy of.

Time to address any obvious changes and see if this supports the quality of your sleep over time.

Recipe 2 – Clearing the Mind

If you find that you carry a lot of to do lists in your head and they come alive at night, a written plan of what you need to remember for tomorrow is a good idea. Maybe spend some time in the evening to do a brain dump.

It will allow you to confidently forget things you may be holding in your memory for the night, knowing it's on the list, it won't be forgotten, and you don't need to keep hold of it.

Recipe 3 – Sleep Routines

Candles, meditation recordings, CBD, sleepy rollerballs, magnesium oil, for example, can all be part of a good sleep routine. Over time, your body and mind will read the signals that it's time to get ready for sleep.

A routine, reading, a bath... anything which is consistent each evening will be useful as will limiting caffeine and screen time, both which awaken the brain into alert mode.

What changes could you make?

Recipe 4 – Move Towards Tired

Are you able to walk or move more in the daytime, to use up energy stored in your body?

If so, what would that look like for you and when are you going to commit to doing so? Be real with yourself here as to what's achievable, as big goals and targets are great, but smaller changes often get us to where we want to be in better time.

Recipe 5 – Conscious Resting

Wakeful rest has a lot of research to show that our bodies replenish in this state. Knowing and enjoying the experience of wakeful rest is a massive changer for people with sleep issues. It can turn frustration and upset into something which can be enjoyed and relaxed into. It can also lead to deep power naps and even deeper sleep.

If awake at night, can you use this time to get to know yourself, your energy, your emotions and your patterns of thinking and worry on a deeper level? This rest may not be sleep, but it is restful, and it is healing for the body.

Wakeful rest/stillness is incredibly nourishing, and the enjoyment of its opportunity will serve you far greater than fighting with a mind that doesn't want to sleep.

Putting your mind to use for inner inquiry will have you feeling far more rested, and you will become more self-aware in the process.

♡

For Your Notes...

MESS & CLUTTER

The tiredness with mess is heavy, alluring, real and it robs us of energy.

It creates a noise within its silence, and oh, its harshness of judgement, that's a real killer of joy.

So, what is mess?

Sometimes it's physical clutter in your home, sometimes it's the clothing you hold on to which holds you in the past and sometimes it's the energy of judgement and shame.

You will know if it's mess if it keeps luring you back into criticism of any kind.

Some of the mess is unnoticed and remains harmless, whilst some invites you to sink into a stale sense of boredom and maybe a detachment from feeling energised and creative.

So how do you identify what's mess and what isn't an issue for you?

You listen for the noise and tend to the noisiest first, as this will be the biggest killer of your sense of peace within this subject.

♡

MESS & CLUTTER

Possible indicators and symptoms of mess & clutter (amongst many more)

You repeatedly walk past or bump into areas in your home, car, workplace, wardrobe, and remind yourself that you wanted to clear something, but then repeatedly forget.

You regularly criticise and judge yourself for not sorting an area out.

You avoid being near or around those areas, even if it's a diversion of attention.

You find yourself tired, agitated or with apathy when in the areas which require a little tidy up.

LIFE'S SIMPLE RECIPES

RECIPES FOR MESS & CLUTTER

Recipe 1 – Feeling into Clutter

Recipe 2 – Power Clear-Ups

Recipe 3 – Digital Tidy-Up

Recipe 4 – Letting Go

Recipe 1 – Feeling into Clutter

Stand or sit in a room or an area in your home for a few moments in silence and bring your focus back to you, your body and your energy. Breathe and just be here for a few moments.

After a minute or so, notice if your attention or energy is drawn towards any mess or clutter.

Does this bring up any sense of judgement, annoyance or criticism towards yourself?

Which, if any, feels the heaviest?

Can you commit some time to sort the loudest mess, with the intention to lighten the heaviness it brings up for you?

Recipe 2 – Power Clear-Ups

Power clear-ups can be so effective and setting a timer, for even 5 minutes of undistracted clearing will get things shifted.

This often leads to more than 5 minutes, but if you find it tricky, 5 minutes is a great way to get things cleared, without it feeling too challenging.

Recipe 3 – Digital Tidy-Up

Committing to 5 minutes at a time to clear messages, emails, photos and other things no longer needed from your phone clears heaviness.

The energy in messages holds an emotional charge, most which are attached to a past that no longer needs to be carried around.

Sounds simple?

Try it...it's an energiser for sure!

Recipe 4 – Letting Go

Have a look around your home and notice whether you are holding on to items that give you no joy at all. Items you never notice, look at or pay attention to.

Ask yourself why you hold on to them, and whether you can let them go to someone who will really enjoy them.

The same applies to your wardrobe and clothing.

LIFE'S SIMPLE RECIPES

For Your Notes...

SLOWING DOWN TO GET MORE DONE

Tightness of chest, fuzzy buzzy energy, shortness of breath due to stress, hamster wheel chattery thoughts, searching for peace, a sense of urgent busyness, sometimes close to tears for everything to just stop for a while, but there just isn't the time.

The very notion that you need to do more to get things done is not true. In fact, it can often lead to procrastination, frustration, judgement and overwhelm.

If someone had tried to tell me a while ago that slowing down in our action, and sometimes actually doing nothing, when you have so much to do, actually gets more done, I'd have told them they didn't know what they were talking about. But that's exactly what I'm suggesting here.

♡

Possible indicators and symptoms of not slowing down (amongst many more)

Trying to do more than one thing at a time and not doing any of the tasks very well; feeling forgetful mid- task, feeling rushed, stressed, tearful, anxious and believing it's near impossible to get things done in time.

LIFE'S SIMPLE RECIPES

RECIPES FOR SLOWING DOWN

Recipe 1 – Stop, Pause & Slow Down

Recipe 2 – Slowing Down

Recipe 3 – One Thing at a Time

Recipe 4 – Doing More in Less Time

Recipe 5 – Powerful Mini Pauses

Recipe 1 – Stop, Pause & Slow Down

Obvious one here, but it needs saying...STOP - if you find yourself in overwhelm or even mild panic about how much you must do in a limited amount of time, get a blanket, light a candle, put on some soft music and lay down, undisturbed, eyes closed for a minimum of 15 minutes; 30 minutes is ideal.

This simple act will slow down your energy, your perspective, your thinking and your sense of urgency.

This simple act will give you more clarity, can calm your nervous system and will in fact stretch time itself.

Crazy? It's true, try it...

Recipe 2 – Slowing Down

Slow down...physically slow down.

Slowing the speed in which you move your body will slow your energy as well as your thinking. It will put your nervous system into a calmer state, you will gain more clarity, feel more in control and get more done.

When your body is feeling the stress of rushing around, be that physically or in a racing mind, it produces hormones to speed up your heart rate, raising blood pressure and creating a sensation of urgency. Your body is ready to respond in fight or flight mode, which increases feelings of stress with the come down of tiredness.

When your body is slower, sending signals of relaxation through your parasympathetic system, hormones of safety are produced, which slow down your heart rate, lower your blood pressure

and has been shown to reduce stress – experienced not only in the mind but in the body too.

The simple act of slowing our walking and actions in all the tasks we carry out WILL expand what you're able to do and challenge this rat race mentality and the effects this stress can have not only on your body but in your life.

Recipe 3 – One Thing at a Time

Commit to doing one thing at a time when you have a lot of do, especially when you start to feel overwhelm creeping in.

One thing at a time, with no distraction.

No phone, no checking emails, no social media peek, no other task creeping in.

Focus on one thing at a time and get it done before moving on to another task.

Recipe 4 – Doing More in Less Time

Building and developing confidence, that you CAN get more done without rushing around within the energy of urgency, will slow things down and support your nervous system.

Slowing into tasks will get things completed more quickly and you will feel lighter and more energised.

Dedicate time each day to build this 'slowing down muscle' and see for yourself if this is true.

Recipe 5 – Powerful Mini Pauses

Create some mini pause stops throughout your day. Even 30 seconds will set you up really well for becoming more comfortable with a slower pace. Slow and steady always wins the race, as does tiny little changes and mini steps.

It's about longevity here, not a sprint.

You might enjoy the Yoga Nidra in the Free Resources for this. You'll find a link at the back of the book.

LIFE'S SIMPLE RECIPES

For Your Notes...

SELF-SABOTAGE

Conflict of confidence, a pull towards a passionate desire, found up against the walls of reasons why you're not able to commit. Left in an energy of wanting but never quite achieving.

The essence of this is a belief of not deserving, not good enough, fear and concern around judgement; the most painful of judgement being that towards oneself.

This self-judgement stings and keeps you stuck, sometimes in agony of longing and at other times, in a pool of relief.

A relief that you haven't quite yet got to show yourself to the world.

♡

SELF-SABOTAGE

Possible indicators and symptoms of self-sabotage (amongst many more)

Great plans but never completed, lots of sharing of your dreams with lack of purposeful action. Looking outside at other people's lives wondering how they are achieving what you feel you are not.

Self-doubt, lack of confidence and maybe glimpses of imposter syndrome.

LIFE'S SIMPLE RECIPES

RECIPES FOR SELF-SABOTAGE

Recipe 1 – Hearing Self-Sabotage

Recipe 2 – Do You Want It?

Recipe 3 – There Is No Perfect Time

Recipe 1 – Hearing Self-Sabotage

Name something, a goal if you like that you feel you are in 'self-sabotage' with.

Make a list of the reasons as to why you would like to achieve this goal. What will you gain from it and what will you lose?

List known reluctancies or avoidance to follow through with action to achieve this goal.

What are your gains from not actioning this goal and what will you lose if you do jump into action?

Compare these lists and become aware of both the gains and losses they give to you so that you can decide which you want most.

You can then decide what you want most and what action to take to achieve this, regardless of the feelings and emotions obstructing your actions.

If we wait for the 'right feeling' which is usually a tool of procrastination, we will be waiting a long time.

When we are able to action what we want, regardless of presenting procrastination, we will achieve what we want with much less struggle. The irony huh?

It's either a yes or a no and doesn't require judgement or justification.

It's always a question of yes, or no?

Do I want this or not, and I mean REALLY want it?

Recipe 2 – Do You Want It?

Be honest as to whether you are creating a story or a belief around it not being the right time.

If we truly want something, we do it, so if you're saying to yourself, it's not the right time, you may actually be saying you don't want it enough

Do you want it or not?

A simple yes or no, no judgement or justification needed, this is your life and your choice.

Journal what comes up for you in defence for this reflection.

Recipe 3 – There Is No Perfect Time

Can you get comfortable with an action, regardless of how you are feeling about it, if it takes you towards something you want?

Just as there isn't the right or wrong time for something, there are no right or wrong moods or feelings to have, in order to get started.

Again, it's an honest and simple yes or no.

Find out where the judgement is running the show in either scenario.

LIFE'S SIMPLE RECIPES

For Your Notes...

The Guest House

This being human is a guest house,

Every morning a new arrival.

A joy, a depression, a meanness, some momentary awareness comes as an unexpected visitor.

Welcome and entertain them all!

Even if they're a crowd of sorrows, who violently sweep your house empty of its furniture, still treat each guest honourably.

He may be clearing you out for some new delight.

The dark thought, the shame, the malice, meet them at the door laughing and invite them in.

Be grateful for whoever comes, because each has been sent as a guide from beyond.

Jalaluddin Rumi

JUDGEMENT

A gasping slap, a sharp pain and the hardened ball it leaves in the core of your stomach. Sometimes with sadness of heart and sometimes with shame. Oh, the shame, that stings the most.

Anger of mind, words firing swords, lashing out from the embers which are born from the most painful judgement of all; the one you cast upon yourself, and from which all other judgements are seeded from.

It's so easy to assume and believe that the judgements we have towards other people are about them and not us, but that's just not the case.

If we wake up feeling happy about ourselves, this is the energy we carry into our day and into the conversations we have with ourselves and others too.

If we wake up annoyed, criticising ourselves for something we believe is in the privacy of our own mind, we are very much mistaken.

The next person or people we communicate with will feel this tight energy, or possibly even be inflicted with the weapons fired out from this self-judgement. BOOM, fuel for more self-criticism is ignited, as at some point, you will bring these inflictions back for reflection and pour blame back into your own energy.

The exhausting cycle possibly continues until you decide enough is enough…no more self-judgement.

Then watch what happens to the relationships in your life, as they start to flourish and become more truthful and real.

If you are being overly critical and judgemental towards those in your life, the root cause of this will be in how you are judging yourself.

That's how we challenge this behaviour and end these exhausting and unhealthy ways of being with those we love.

We stop judging ourselves and it's this energy which then feeds all our relationships.

♡

LIFE'S SIMPLE RECIPES

Possible indicators and symptoms of self-judgement (amongst many more)

You are overly critical about people and situations, and you share this criticism often within your conversations.

You like to control situations and get agitated if someone isn't doing or being how you would like them to be.

You are easily agitated by other people, you put them down as well as yourself.

You feel shame, are easily pulled into arguments and frequently get annoyed with yourself.

You are quick to put yourself down for making little mistakes, are often snappy, sad and tired.

RECIPES FOR JUDGEMENT

Recipe 1 – Daily Check In

Recipe 2 – Acknowledge What You Like About YOU

Recipe 3 – Noticing Criticism

Recipe 1 – Daily Check In

When you wake up, can you give yourself 5 minutes to ask these very simple questions, and be open and receptive to YOUR own feedback?

This is about trust, and if you can support yourself with what you hear, then you can more easily build a kind relationship with yourself and the world you live in.

Sometimes you can adjust your day and other times you can't.

Being aware of how you are is what is most supportive for you in your day.

So, here are the questions to ask, in a quiet space when you awake - You can journal your answers to these questions or simply reflect in the space of quiet stillness.

1. How am I today?

2. How's my energy today?

3. How are my emotions today?

4. How am I feeling today?

5. What actions can I take to support this feedback and how does that practically look for me today?

6. What 1 thing can I do today for me which is kind? What kind act will I commit to, as today's priority for me?

You might enjoy my regular Tuesday Check-in for this. You'll find a link to a sample video in the Free Resources at the back of the book.

Recipe 2 – Acknowledge What You Like About YOU

Can you make a list of things you like about yourself? It may start with one thing, or it may fill a page.

Noticing and holding ourselves in a truthful energy of compliments will soften judgement.

It may be about how you look, values you hold, something you've done well. Anything, as long as it's a true representation of how you feel.

Write it down and acknowledge yourself for it/these things.

Pause and breathe these acknowledgments into your awareness and body. Hold it there for a few moments, allowing full integration into your cells and into your acceptance.

Recipe 3 – Noticing Criticism

Can you bring awareness to the little tuts and criticisms you make towards yourself when, for example, you leave something behind, drop something, forget what you were saying or doing?

Noticing these automatic criticisms is powerful and supports us in questioning, and maybe challenging the stronger, more obvious ones.

If you went around yelling and telling someone they were stupid for dropping keys, forgetting items or saying the wrong thing, you'd be very aware of the damage and reactions it could cause.

You would see the shrinking or defensiveness in their energy very clearly, and this shrinking of you is no different, and is just as harmful or triggering.

If you can pause before automatic criticisms show themselves, you'll start to see where you are constantly putting yourself down and you have the choice to change this unconscious habit.

Once you stop this behaviour, you will start to see that you are less inclined to share these judgements towards others in your life.

Remember, our relationships with others start with how we speak to and about ourselves.

JUDGEMENT

For Your Notes...

RESENTMENT

Anger, fire erupting, aching rage, annoyance at someone, wrapped in obsessive thinking and circles of something not being fair.

Difficulty or refusal to see the reality of a bigger picture, leading to a destruction and overwhelming sense of lost joy.

Resentment, a human form of jealousy, expectancy, being let down or owed something. Moments of not being happy for your own or somebody else's situation, which then causes you emotional pain and guilt. A muddled sense of resentful emotions, which seems to have a mind of their own.

When we do not have an open and truthful relationship with ourselves around our emotions and situation in our life, we can sometimes grab onto controlling thoughts or drift into comparison, judgement, unspoken pain and hurt.

We can become frozen within inaction, moving us further away from what we think we want in our lives.

You may see others living how you want to be living and it's tricky to be happy for them because you are annoyed with yourself. A breakdown in communication, assumptions, not wanting to communicate, wanting to compete even.

RESENTMENT

If you're feeling frustration, annoyance, anger, jealousy and/or shame, the emotions projected outwards around this resentment could well be indicative of your own punitive measures towards yourself and your life.

That's what's leading you to push away, to back off, to get defensive, to react to somebody else's life in a way that is retractive, when most likely, they know nothing about it. It's a killer of joy!

How about, rather than looking to what's lacking for you, through what you feel somebody else has, maybe look at where you're not allowing yourself to have that which you see and are seeking in another?

There is a beautiful Ancient Nahuatic Blessing found in Closing Thoughts at the back of this book, which you may find supportive for this.

♡

Possible indicators and symptoms of held and problematic resentment (amongst many more)

Gossiping, pulling away from somebody you're close to, avoidance, isolating yourself from people or situations.

Getting angry, procrastinating, obsessed annoyance, frustration.

Immature communication, not being able to speak your natural truth.

Not being pleased or able to celebrate other people for what they have, leading to a dislike or discomfort of/with self and others due to this.

RECIPES FOR RESENTMENT

Recipe 1 - Resentments

Recipe 2 – Fears And Worries

Recipe 3 – Pausing Within Emotions

Recipe 1 - Resentments

Can you be truthful with yourself about any resentments you are holding?

Problematic resentments seem to crop up when there is an emotional attachment or connection to someone involved or a repeating theme.

So, it's maybe not about a situation at all, but more a perceived loss or fear of change within a relationship dynamic?

Is there a sense of lack or a change you don't want to see? Is this sense of lack or change true?

Are you creating what you don't want by withdrawing?

Are you creating the resentment and heaviness with assumptions or worry?

RESENTMENT

Shining a light on the truth of your emotions, without judgement or criticism but with interest, IS powerful.

You can't change and soften your energy without a willingness and openness to see these truths.

If you are casting a judging eye over it, then you're just going to hide it further.

So, let's get the judgement and criticism out of the way and take an honest view.

Recipe 2 – Fears And Worries

Be truthful with yourself about where you have any fears/worries around these resentments and listen to them.

Hearing yourself is powerful, it's OK to feel the pain, and it's a falseness to think we can live in a constant world of acceptance and happiness.

We can live within a constant feeling of being grounded and balanced, with a peaceful foundation, when we allow ourselves to see and feel what is happening for us.

Once we hear what our concerns, pain, fears and worries are about, these resentments can slowly lighten and even transform into compassion.

Recipe 3 – Pausing Within Emotions

When you feel the waves, the pulls and the tugs of resentment which splash and crash into your stomach, flooding into your mind and knocking you over in your sense of openness, can you pause within that emotion?

Can you give that situation some space before reacting, before speaking to anybody about it, before doing anything with it? Can you allow it to be there for a while?

Your reaction may be to squirm or push the emotions you feel away.

Can you be with them or a little while?

Can you journal the emotions, the fears, the worries to be able to hear the truth?

What's going on for you here, right now?

LIFE'S SIMPLE RECIPES

For Your Notes...

COMMITMENT

The desire to make change seems strong but there is no plan of action, leading to yet another broken promise to yourself.

Apathy and lethargy replace a short-lived enthusiasm and trust in your ability is broken once again. Nothing changes.

It's easy to declare change or commitment to something you would like, but without a plan of action, it remains a wish.

So often, steps towards something are way too big and unrealistic, creating a sense of exhaustion; or it becomes too overwhelming to begin. Excuses are created instead of movement into action.

When we decide we would like to make a change in our life, it's important that we start from where we currently are and move forward from there.

Trying to start from a place in the future is unrealistic and likely to have us fail.

♡

COMMITMENT

Possible indicators and symptoms of commitment issues (amongst many more)

Repeatedly planning projects and declaring good intentions, but they are short-lived, amount to half measures or nothing at all, are pushed aside or forgotten about.

A lack of trust in oneself is created, self-annoyance follows the high of declarations, as you fall back into the comfort of staying in the same routines.

LIFE'S SIMPLE RECIPES

RECIPES FOR COMMITMENT

Recipe 1 – Getting Clear

Recipe 2 – Making a Plan

Recipe 3 – Accountability

Recipe 4 – Visual Support & Reminders

Recipe 5 – Declaration of Commitment

Recipe 1 – Getting Clear

If you decide you want to start a project or get committed with something, can you:

1. Make a list as to why you want this
2. Determine where you are now in the process
3. Decide what the next step/s will be
4. Be truthful as to what barriers or excuses you may make when you become tired or too busy

Being clear around this means you can plan to support yourself when it feels challenging.

Recipe 2 – Making a Plan

Making a bigger plan can work for some people, especially if you're motivated by the actions you take.

If this doesn't work for you, it can help to break the process down into stages and plan each step.

Sometimes, a tick box or reward at various milestones can be a great motivator.

Recipe 3 – Accountability

Can you pair up with an accountability buddy to plan to prioritise a date and time to make a start to get things moving forward?

Sometimes, pairing up with someone who is working on their own goals can be helpful.

The goals and actions can be different, as it's the space you create together that is the container for both of you.

Be honest with each other as to how it's going, where the challenges are, and what you are most likely to want to avoid or procrastinate on? This joint honesty can be not only liberating but powerful in creating the change that we want.

Recipe 4 – Visual Support & Reminders

Making a visual chart or list of a weekly commitment plan can help you to allocate some time and space, so that you can't use the excuse of not having time.

If a week feels too unrealistic, challenging or overwhelming, planning a day at a time may be better.

A little planning can go a long way, especially in small chunks that are manageable.

If you are someone who writes action plans and forgets to look at them, can you put them in a place you have a frequent view of, such as the fridge, by the kettle or on the mantlepiece?

Recipe 5 – Declaration of Commitment

Can you sign a declaration to yourself for your commitment, stating your 'why's, 'how's and what you will gain from completing this task?

An example of a declaration can be found and used on the following page. This is also available to download in my Free Resources. Find more information in the links at the back of the book.

COMMITMENT

I commit to (write your task)

I want to do this because (write your 'why's)

I plan to achieve this by (write 'how's)

By doing this my life improves (state how)

If things get tricky, I will support myself (write how)

I am there for myself because I deserve to have balance in my life.

Sign: Date:

LIFE'S SIMPLE RECIPES

For Your Notes...

PART TWO

Building an honest relationship with yourself

LIFE'S SIMPLE RECIPES

Going Deeper

Now we've cleaned our metaphorical kitchen, let's go a little deeper...

So, we have established reliable foundations for balanced living in Part One.

Part One offered a continual check in with yourself, with solid maintenance for balance.

Part Two goes deeper and supports you to build a stronger and truthful relationship with yourself. It offers space for silent reflection and uses the same structure for continuity. It is a great place to explore once your foundations are holding you well.

If you find you are feeling tired, overwhelmed and busy, pop back to Part One to see if there's a foundational recipe worth spending time with. It could be as simple as drinking enough water, which seems the simplest of all, but often one of the hardest things to remember.

You know how the flow of the exploration feels, so you can dive straight in.

Part Two will look at:

- Nervous system calling
- More balance in what you love
- Safety
- Kindness as a value
- Cluttered beliefs, thinking and habits
- Loneliness
- Being comfortable with quiet
- Unplugging
- Being uncontactable

I hope you enjoy your time pondering these.

♡

NERVOUS SYSTEM CALLING

Such an intelligent system for translating what's happening in our perception, beliefs and experiences, for our body to feel, process and communicate to us.

It offers such a gift of friendship, but are we open to knowing its wisdom or is it a stranger?

Why is it that when we feel a hint of overwhelm, stress, anxiety or upset, we try to blame, control or change our environment and external experiences?

Why do so many of us have a default to alter our outside experiences in an attempt to avoid or look at what's happening from within our emotions and feelings?

I believe that this is because we aren't used to, aren't comfortable with or don't like the sensations or feedback our emotions signal to our body. It feels uncomfortable and so we divert our attention elsewhere and label the experience as the cause of our discomfort.

External factors have a massive impact on how we feel or react, and this is very real and deserves the tenderness and time to explore.

However, what can help us to manage our reactions in a more consistently balanced way, is to know what supports feelings of safety as well as what triggers agitation in our nervous system.

When our nervous system is triggered, often we will move further towards focusing on these triggers. For example, if like me the News and war reporting is a known trigger, when feeling vulnerable, you may look at the News in hope to find that everything is peaceful in the world.

If it's all peaceful, peace is felt in that reassurance, but if there's more disruption, it takes us even deeper into the symptoms felt from these known triggers.

Our sense of safety can become dependent on external forces, which is never certain and will land us in emotional trouble for sure.

What is more reliable and more truthful is to look towards what soothes and supports our nervous system, what we enjoy, what brings us a sense of calm and/or joy and what helps us to feel safe.

In time, these things may become a natural default in holding ourselves in balance, as opposed to reactionary actions of doing.

For this to happen, the habit of holding ourselves will need to have become a path well-trodden.

♡

Possible indicators and symptoms of a stressed nervous system
(amongst many more)

Snappy, tired, inability to think clearly, wanting to isolate, jumpiness, nervous, alert to danger, reactive, headaches, body pain, insomnia, exhaustion, rejecting the thoughts of anyone asking anything of us, dread, doom and often despair.

LIFE'S SIMPLE RECIPES

Recipes for Soothing a Nervous System

Recipe 1 – Nervous System Soothers

Recipe 2 – Nervous System Triggers

Recipe 3 – Sandwich of Support

Recipe 1 – Nervous System Soothers

Make a list of things you know will help you to feel relaxed, calm, happy and safe. These may include a walk in nature, a lay down with gentle music and a soft blanket. Watching the birds or sky out of the window, having a cuppa whilst snuggling with a pet or just enjoying the peace and quiet etc. The quieter the activity, away from others as well as electronic devices, the more soothing it will be for your nervous system. The less input coming in, the less reactionary output.

Making a list really helps us to remember what works for us, because often, when stressed, we will forget, especially if this isn't how we are used to caring for ourselves.

Recipe 2 – Nervous System Triggers

Make a list of all the things which you know are triggers of stress and/or overwhelm for you.

It may be, as mentioned before, the News, or it could be too much time on social media/screens, spending time with certain people or going around in circles of conversation. It could be conversations which you find challenging, such as politics, or being with forcefully opinionated people who like to overshare.

Knowing what some of these triggers are can really help us to know where we can pull back from, when feeling overwhelmed.

Recipe 3 – Sandwich of Support

If you are going to be around or within known triggers, can you plan to sandwich these occasions with some soothers before and afterwards?

Building in ways to look out for us, in a way which isn't externally dependent, helps us to build healthy personal boundaries, especially when life feels stressful.

We can't control what happens around us, but we can support ourselves to feel better equipped to weather the storms and to recover after them.

Regulating our nervous system through everyday choices, which don't take much time, don't cost money and don't involve anyone else, is powerful for building personal resilience.

We don't avoid, we love ourselves through.

That's empowerment and it comes from knowing ourselves and making our nervous system a priority in our lives.

♡

For Your Notes...

MORE BALANCE IN WHAT YOU LOVE

Watching others doing wonderful things which make them seem happy, with a felt sense of being distant from feeling that happiness yourself.

Not noticing or taking into consideration the time and commitment they may have made to bring this into their own busy life and not accepting your own invitation and freedom to do the same for yourself.

A belief of being too busy, too tired or too disinterested…you watch on in hope to feel the same way without changing a thing.

How often do you compare your life to others who seem happy and balanced, yet you never really question how they are creating their life through their actions, or what you can change in your own life to feel more of this lighter energy.

It's never about what someone else has, it is more about you and what you feel you don't have.

What others have, you have no control or influence over; what you have, you can most definitely do something about.

♡

Possible indicators and symptoms of not having a healthy balance of things you enjoy in your life (amongst many more)

Lots of comparisons with other people's lives, low mood, tiredness, apathy, criticism, judgement, overly self-concerned; obsessive thinking around what other people have, neglect of self-care/love, poor nutritional habits and jealousy to name a few.

LIFE'S SIMPLE RECIPES

MORE BALANCE IN WHAT YOU LOVE

RECIPES FOR BRINGING MORE OF WHAT YOU LOVE INTO YOUR LIFE

Recipe 1 - What Do You Love?

Recipe 2 – What One Thing?

Recipe 3 – Reflection & Planning

Recipe 4 – Knowing Our Neutralisers

Recipe 5 – Habits, People Pleasing and Clarity

Recipe 6 – Progress NOT Perfection

Recipe 1 - What Do You Love?

Making a list of things you would LOVE more of in your life can be helpful for allowing you to see what you can easily and effortlessly incorporate into your life

It can help you see which require little effort and which may require a little planning.

Recipe 2 – What One Thing?

Can you commit to doing one thing EVERYDAY that you love?

Building on this one thing, in a present and conscious way can become a powerful part of your life, a great habit to nourish and doesn't have to be time dependent.

Recipe 3 – Reflection & Planning

Can you take 5 minutes at the end of the week, to reflect how your week felt with things you love planned and included?

What will you plan to bring into the week to come?

Recipe 4 – Knowing Our Neutralisers

Can you make a list of things which are emotionally challenging for you and that you really don't enjoy?

Things which feel like they neutralise the energy from things you love?

You'll feel the difference, one will energise whilst the other depletes.

Often, we can't avoid or change things we don't like, nor should we, but we can acknowledge the impact it may be having on us.

Knowing this impact, we can decide whether we are happy with the balance of how things are.

Recipe 5 – Habits, People Pleasing and Clarity

Look at the list of things you love and things which deplete your joy (Recipe 1 and 4 in this chapter).

Be clear and present with these lists and check that there aren't things on your list which are purely there from being a habit of what you think you like. I mention this because we evolve, and often things we love evolve too, yet we haven't checked in as to whether we still enjoy those activities or whether they are in fact a habit no longer loved. If you notice this, remove them from your list, as this list is for things that lighten your energy.

If you notice you have listed things you do that are more about other people's pleasure rather than your own, then I would suggest taking these off too.

Of course, you will be part of other people's pleasure, but this list is purely for you and what absolutely nourishes you fully.

Recipe 6 – Progress NOT Perfection

If you miss a commitment made to yourself for something you love, listen without judgement into why you aren't allowing yourself this pleasure.

Go gentle…it's about awareness here and not punishment. Awareness leads to change; judgement can lead to inaction and unnecessary stress.

For Your Notes...

SAFETY

The place where you feel most vibrantly alive, able and empowered. Where you can nudge the walls of discomfort with the knowing that you are able to handle what bounces back. The place where you want to take action, even in doubt, because you have confidence in yourself to enter unknown territory…

Safety, a fundamental ingredient in being able to truly step into and live from your own power, desires and authentic life.

So, here's the thing. To be able to share and live your life authentically, with all of you present, even the bits you don't think you like, it's important, not essential but important, to feel safe in your environment, in your body, in your mind and in your choices.

Often, when we hear the word safety, we can, on default, pull our attention towards threats to our physical self/life. When we don't have confidence in our own abilities to manage our life, concerns of physical threats can be heightened and overwhelm increased.

Another layer to feeling safe is having confidence in the way we look after, know and protect ourselves. How we support ourselves through our own reactions, from our own beliefs and conditioning…and at times from the muddles we can find ourselves in due to all the above.

SAFETY

Do you know what safety looks like for you? Are your conditions for feeling safe strongly attached to other people in your life or world events? It's worth a look to see some of the foundations you've laid for yourself around the energy of safety in your life.

♡

Possible indicators and symptoms of limiting beliefs around your safety
(amongst many more)

You feel like you need to be with other people to go and do things you enjoy, a reluctancy to try new things goes deeper than general shyness, you seek advice from others around your health or life decisions, rather than trusting your own; you are in a state of nervousness or anxiety a lot of the time when outside familiarity, you live within the same patterns of behaviour, barely touching the edges of your comfort zone due to not feeling confident enough to be able to cope; you worry about world events and have a tendency to catastrophise your future thinking.

RECIPES FOR FEELING SAFE

Recipe 1 – Feeling Safe

Recipe 2 – Feeling the Weight

Recipe 1 – Feeling Safe

Time for pen and paper…these questions are written so that you can get to know yourself a little deeper, and as always, this is achieved with much more ease when we are curious rather than judgemental. When we can hold these questions in a loving energy to get to know someone incredibly precious…YOU!

So, the questions:

1. Can you think back to times in your life when you felt incredibly confident and able?

2. How did life look and feel for you then? Be as descriptive as possible and really feel into the energy of those times.

3. How is life different now to the above remembered?

4. Are there things either present now or missing from before, which you feel has affected your ability to feel safety in your daily life?

5. Have you grown attachments and conditions of safety to the belief that certain people, places or things need to be present?
   If so, what have these people, places or things given to you for you to feel safe?
   It's helpful to not hold back here and to get everything down for a proper look.

6. Do your realisations hold truth or are they beliefs you have picked up and firmly owned? Have there been times in your life when you've felt safe without these beliefs?

7. Are you OK to have these beliefs as such a big part of your sense of safe?

Recipe 2 – Feeling the Weight

Can you take a nature walk or sit somewhere private and beautiful in nature, to be with what you may have discovered in the previous recipe?

Can you spend time with this to feel into the weight you've been carrying for things needing to be a certain way for you to feel safe?

Is there anything you can let go of or loosen a little around this?

SAFETY

For Your Notes...

KINDNESS AS A VALUE

Strong, trusted, gentle yet bold too.

An unshakeable advocacy, fluid in nature and loving in essence.

A gentle touch when tenderness is asked for and a firmness of intention when stuck.

Kindness isn't always light and soft, sometimes it's required to be firm and direct...But it will always have best interests at the core of its expression, when called upon in so many beautifully felt ways.

Kindness has many shades, and a courage so deep that it can cut through any fears which challenge its integrity.

Bringing kindness home to us isn't often spoken about, but it is a fundamental underpinning of a balanced and happy life. Of course it is. Life thrives on kindness.

So, doesn't it make sense to own and live our own life through the core of our own kindness towards ourselves? Afterall, we can't truly share the energy of kindness with another or towards life, when it's not ignited by the heart pulse of kindness being towards ourselves.

♡

Possible indicators and symptoms of the absence of kindness towards ourselves (amongst many more)

Argumentative, nitpicking, gossiping, criticism, unhappiness as a regular baseline, overly focused upon egoic-self, absent minded, an inability to remain present, self-anger, upset or even hatred, often showing itself as this exact energy towards others, whether vocalised or kept private.

LIFE'S SIMPLE RECIPES

RECIPES FOR KINDNESS

Recipe 1 - How Does Kindness Look for You?

Recipe 2 – What Feels Unkind to You?

Recipe 3 – Shifting Towards More Kindness

Recipe 4 – How Do You Offer Yourself Kindness?

Recipe 5 – Daily Acts of Kindness

Recipe 1 - How Does Kindness Look for You?

Finding out what kindness means to you is an important part of being kind. You can't do something as an act of kindness for yourself if you don't know how that might look or what it is.

Kindness means so many things for different people, so making a list and discovering what it means for you will make it easier to act upon and feel the benefits of.

Some actions may look like kindness for one person but feel unkind for another, so we find out what it looks like for us and share this with ourselves.

Make a list so that you can remind yourself when you forget.

Recipe 2 – What Feels Unkind to You?

The same discovery as the previous recipe, but this time let's look at what feels unkind, so that we are aware not to inflict that upon ourselves.

Some people find a firm talking to is motivating and a kind holding, whilst for someone else, it can feel abusive.

Know what feels unkind for you and be mindful around this.

Make a list of things or ways you sometimes act towards yourself which feel unkind.

Recipe 3 – Shifting Towards More Kindness

Look to see how your balance towards yourself sits between kindness and unkind.

Have you discovered anything new and are there any changes or alternatives you'd like to consider or bring for more reflection? If so, what are they? And what could these changes look like in practical terms?

Recipe 4 – How Do You Offer Yourself Kindness?

Being aware of things you like about yourself, and the ways in which you offer yourself kindness can be powerful. It can highlight gaps too, so look at this with gentleness.

Can you list things you like about yourself and how you offer yourself kindness?

You might enjoy my regular Tuesday Check-in for this. You'll find a link to a sample video in the Free Resources at the back of the book.

Recipe 5 – Daily Acts of Kindness

Making it a daily priority to bring kindness towards yourself is undeniably powerful. It has potential to significantly move your life towards more balance.

With that in mind, can you commit to a daily check in, as in Part One or similar?

If you would like to commit to a daily self-check in, doing so before you get out of bed each morning is ideal, but any time will be of great benefit.

It's a powerful action to decide on one thing you WILL do today to show yourself the energy of kindness. It can be as small as making sure you drink enough water or as big as putting a boundary down in an area that has been asking for one for a long time.

KINDNESS AS A VALUE

For Your Notes...

Interfere

Interfere, sounds to me like into fear,

Wow, is that what I do when I interfere.

And then, do I not trust that you can find your own way home.

Do I not trust you.

Do I not see your magnificence and genius, to solve this on your own.

Do I not see all the love that shines from your very being,

And all the love that surrounds you.

Do I not trust in all of this.

So do I go into fear and then feel I have to interfere,

Not for you but for ME!

So, what can I do?

Or maybe, what if I could just be, and go into love.

Because this is where I trust.

This is where I really see you, in all your magnificence,

And in all your love.

And I know you know your own genius,

And your own way home.

So, from now on, I will choose to go into love.

Yes, instead of interfering, I will now open into loving.

Jeanette Tuppen

CLUTTERED THINKING, BELIEFS AND HABITS

Such a deep-seated longing, a craving almost, and an orchestra of noise in your thinking, causing a tension in your body.

Unrest, unfulfilled and if quite honest, a little lost.

Just as we can get lost in the clutter and mess of physical items, the clutter within our own beliefs, habits and thinking can feel the messiest of all.

It can have us feeling lost in a seeming prison of gut-wrenching struggle at times. Struggle not to care so deeply, to feel so attached, rejected, ignored and unappreciated.

These beliefs and feelings are powerful and real; however, they are orchestrated by our own innocent doing and therefore, can also be untangled by us alone.

Sometimes these habits of thought and behaviour are a default of a well-trodden path that at some point never existed.

So, if you don't like the path, it's worth some effort and committed action to start creating a new one. A newly trodden path without such clutter, mess and heavy noise.

♡

Possible indicators and symptoms of energetic mess and clutter (amongst many more)

Overly critical of others, be that vocally or private.

Actions led by a desire for others to notice or validate; valuing other's opinions over your own; controlling personality traits to mask anxiety, unstable boundaries within relationships, leading to exhaustion, over excitement and burnout.

LIFE'S SIMPLE RECIPES

Recipes for Cluttered Thinking, Beliefs and Habits

Recipe 1 – Journalling Emotional Themes

Recipe 2 – Whose Responsibility Is This?

Recipe 3 – Do They Know Who You Think They Are?

Recipe 4 – People Pleasing Is to Please Ourselves

Recipe 5 – Moving On from Cluttered Thinking

Recipe 6 – Subtle Expectations

Recipe 1 – Journalling Emotional Themes

Be real and honest with yourself, no one else is listening or judging; so, trust yourself to write down all your thoughts, emotions, reactions, anger, hatred, jealousy, vulnerabilities and rejections you have about an emotionally fuelled or messy situation.

Not being real and honest here is judging yourself. You can't build a trusty relationship based on judgement.

So, without the energy of judgement, get everything out and seen with this writing and then destroy it.

The destroying it straight away will not only allow you to feel safe in this exploration, but will dissolve the energy of your words too.

Recipe 2 – Whose Responsibility Is This?

Identify what responsibilities you are putting into the hands and life of another for your own sense of happiness.

Question whether you've shared with them that you feel they are responsible for this aspect of your life.

Are you even on the same page with this?

Recipe 3 – Do They Know Who You Think They Are?

Where there is a messy relationship, list how you view this person. List the beliefs, values or attributes you feel they have and that you may feel let down by.

Reflect on whether your view of them is how they know themselves to be, or whether it's something you've made up yourself.

So often, the conflict in relationship struggles is around who we need them to be for us, rather than who they truly are.

No one can live up to what we want them to be nor should they, especially when they have no idea as to how we view them.

To identify where we are doing this WILL clear so much emotional and mental clutter of past, present and for the future too.

Recipe 4 – People Pleasing Is to Please Ourselves

Taking responsibility for where we people please AND where we stay in relationships for the purpose of filling a need in us, is another area to be brave enough to look at.

Making a list of noisy relationships in your life and being honest as to what you gain and lose from these relationships is a great use of your time.

The awareness on this can influence future choices you make and bring more balance into your life.

Recipe 5 – Moving On from Cluttered Thinking

What changes can you make to move on from some of your cluttered thinking?

Listing the noisiest is the best place to start if you're looking for the biggest changes.

Focusing into a less emotional theme is useful if the noise is a little too much at this point.

Be clear on what the noise is and what responsibility and action you will take/make to change the energy.

Recipe 6 – Subtle Expectations

Where there is a lot of noise and frustration around a certain relationship dynamic, list what is upsetting you and look at where your expectations or unspoken needs are fuelling issues?

For Your Notes...

LONELINESS

'An uncomfortableness with being alone with yourself. A belief that you are not enough, that you need others in your life to give it meaning and that others offer you more than you offer to yourself. That's a difficult belief and way of living to remain imprisoned by'.

Being uncomfortable when alone is true for many people, because they've invested way more time away from knowing themselves. All in an attempt to know themselves through the filter and feedback of another.

It's way too overcomplicated and will always lead to a sense of isolation, especially when others aren't able to meet our expectations or demands we put on them, or their feedback isn't what we want to hear either.

So, what do we do?

We invest our loneliness time in getting to know ourselves, as in the essence of who we are and what we seem to be seeking from others. To question whether we can be that for ourselves and not be dependent on others for our own internal needs.

How?

We make time with ourselves a priority.

There can't be loneliness if time alone is a beautiful opportunity of connection and getting to know oneself on a deeper level. How often do you say you don't have time for yourself? How often do you feel lonely?

If you feel lonely, you have time for yourself.

Being an advocate and loving friend to yourself will change your life and will challenge most beliefs and experiences of loneliness.

♡

Possible indicators and symptoms of loneliness (amongst many more)

Sadness, not feeling heard, heart yearning but not always sure why. Excessive nostalgia, withdrawing when wanting connection and then feeling isolated. Judging how others have forgotten you, often unable to appreciate the busyness of other people lives. Tiredness, weakened immunity, negative self-talk and low mood, anxiety and the seeking of validation from others.

RECIPES FOR LONELINESS

Recipe 1 – Time Alone

Recipe 2 – Asking Questions of Yourself

Recipe 3 – What One Thing?

Recipe 4 – A Date with You

Recipe 1 – Time Alone

Can you make a commitment to having time with you, a date even; time given to get to know yourself with a deep interest?

When I say yourself, I am referring to the real you, you who often holds back saying or doing things in case it's seen as not good enough.

This real you is the you who people pleases and maybe hasn't given much time for reflection about why this happens, especially if it's to the detriment of your own happiness.

This isn't about the ego self, it's about the more private self which you may not have shared with many others. Quite possibly because you're unaware as to who you are under all the layers of protection and expectations?

LONELINESS

When we meet someone new to our lives, we enjoy getting to know their ways and we are open, intrigued and hold the energy of lightness around it.

Getting to know someone isn't usually a heavy and intense experience, it's usually a light and enjoyable one.

Can you apply the same intrigue, openness and light energy in getting to know yourself?

This isn't a heavy head driven thing to be with, it's an opening and accepting into what we find and know about ourselves.

It's also a noticing when there is energy of emotion which squirms, blushes, shames and judges.

Sometimes getting to know ourselves is something we do alone, privately and sometimes with support of a coach, therapist or friend.

The key is making the focus on getting to know yourself a priority and supporting this to be a light, gentle and real experience.

If judgement is there, acknowledge it of course, but that doesn't mean you have to believe and take sides with that judgement.

Recipe 2 – Asking Questions of Yourself

Can you commit to noticing something new about yourself every day?

Can you ask yourself questions, such as journal prompts to get to know yourself on a deeper level?

Questions to ask could explore what your dreams and aspirations are, what makes you happy or sad, what you like or dislike, passions, fears, and favourite places to visit. There is so much to discover about yourself.

Recipe 3 – What One Thing?

What one small thing can you do today to be a really good friend to yourself?

Recipe 4 – A Date with YOU

Can you plan and make a date, some time to enjoy and focus on some time alone? Time alone to be an incredibly nurturing experience, where loneliness just can't exist?

LIFE'S SIMPLE RECIPES

For Your Notes...

BEING COMFORTABLE WITH QUIETNESS

The avoidance of stillness, when the world feels too noisy.

Just 30 mins is enough to wrap you up in a blanket of wisdom, awareness, clarity and more spacious energy but it seems too much.

The noise weighing heavy on your chest, whirling in your mind and nauseating your stomach.

Oh, the friend of 30 minutes, why are you so hard to be with?

When overwhelmed and stressed, the mind kicks in to find solutions as well as problems and often bumps into other scenarios, which add to your sense of unease.

The mind is telling your nervous system that there's an issue, a danger, and that action is needed to bring you into safety and/or balance.

Adrenaline is released to support action needed and the world feels noisier.

The core of the search is for peace, yet that is often the last action we take.

I decided that letting go of the need to think when in times of doubt is a powerful philosophy to live by.

There is an audio in my Free Resources that can support you in this. You'll find a link at the back of the book.

♡

Possible indicators and symptoms of a noisy living (amongst many more)

Tension headaches, moving from one task to another, rarely completing the list you've made; feelings of dread, tightness of breathing, rushing about; avoiding situations due to lack of mental capacity; a persistent desire for life to slow down, yet something stops you from doing so.

LIFE'S SIMPLE RECIPES

RECIPES FOR BEING MORE COMFORTABLE WITH QUIET

Recipe 1 – Making Time to Pause

Recipe 2 – A Quiet Cuppa

Recipe 3 – Turning Down the Noise

Recipe 1 – Making Time to Pause

Let's get straight in the uncomfortableness of pausing to see what's happening for you.

Plan either 30 minutes or an hour to put aside and sit in silence.

You decide what you can manage best.

No books, music or distraction.

It can be inside or outside, eyes open or closed.

The only aim here is to see how you interact with the space of you when you're alone, without distraction.

No judgement here, just a curious conversation between you and stillness.

You may notice heavy as well as light thoughts, and at the end of the pause, you will have forgotten pretty much all of the content of your thinking.

This activity supports us to feel our thinking as a flow of energy that passes and returns.

It also supports us to know the absolute okay ness of not acting or doing anything when thoughts pull us into wanting to take immediate action.

We wonder why we are exhausted a lot of the time, and often we haven't realised that we are trying to action all our thoughts (60,000 a day approx.).

It isn't necessary nor possible!

Recipe 2 – A Quiet Cuppa

Pop the Kettle on, wait for it to boil without walking off, looking at your phone or finding a mental distraction.

Get your mug and your choice of drink.

Notice the smells and textures of your chosen drink, and whilst it brews, allow yourself this time to STOP.

Once you have your cuppa, go sit somewhere you love and enjoy your drink, with maybe a magazine, book or view of the garden; but leave your phone alone.

Notice how your body and mind feel after these 20/30 minutes and notice any ripples it creates in your day.

Recipe 3 – Turning Down the Noise

If you usually have music or the radio on when you travel or walk somewhere, can you turn it off some of the time and just be with yourself, no distraction?

Can you be with yourself, noticing whether it feels nice, uncomfortable, strange or relaxing?

Turning down the external noise is a great start for those not used to or uncomfortable with their own company…and when I say own, I mean without distractions.

LIFE'S SIMPLE RECIPES

For Your Notes...

UNPLUGGING

Not enough hours in the day, rushing and habitually stopping to fulfil a dopamine hit; sometimes followed with an annoyance that time has passed again.

Lost in screen time with your nervous system at the mercy of another blow.

It really isn't that long ago that unplugging was even in our vocabulary, yet now it's something on most people's minds.

Phones, tablets and PC's have opened our world up enormously, which is a wonderful thing UNLESS it makes life for you smaller and less meaningful.

This is where it's important to look and assess how this is for us, if we are to bring more balance and flow into our life.

Phones are incredibly addictive; we know this and that is why original inventors didn't allow their children and employees' access to them.

Why? Because they can create a virtual reality of experience and a 'living of life' through a rectangular object, rarely looking up to ask where it is enriching life and where it is stealing it away from under your very nose.

♡

Possible indicators and symptoms of being too plugged in (amongst many more)

Habitually reaching for a device without it being an intentional action. Tired eyes, busy mind, distracted, lonely, yearning something, apathetic, losing time in the day, irritability and possibly comparison syndrome kicking in.

LIFE'S SIMPLE RECIPES

RECIPES FOR UNPLUGGING

Recipe 1 – What You'd Like to Make Time For

Recipe 2 – Plan Some Time to Unplug

Recipe 3 – Enjoy Sharing Unplugged Time

Recipe 1 – What You'd Like to Make Time For

Make a list of the things you would like to include more of in your life, such as hobbies, seeing friends or activities, and list the time needed to bring these activities into your day.

An example may be 30 minutes to read a magazine with an uninterrupted cuppa.

Reflect on the reasons you give to yourself around the not having time for these hobbies/activities.

Then, be honest with yourself as to how long you spend with your phone/tablet/PC.

Become aware of the choices you are making here.

Recipe 2 – Plan Some Time to Unplug

Decide on a comfortable amount of time that you feel you can unplug for and put it in your diary.

Have a date with yourself enjoying something you love to do, totally unplugged.

Time with you, for you, and enjoyed by you alone.

Recipe 3 – Enjoy Sharing Unplugged Time

Buddy up with a friend or family member who also wants to unplug and be accountable to each other for this commitment.

Let close ones know you are unplugging and take this time to enjoy the peace and often forgotten relationship of time without a device.

Share time with likeminded people, who also have an interest in appreciating time away from tech distractions and unnecessary noise.

For Your Notes...

BEING UNCONTACTABLE

A twinge of uncomfortableness with a dashing of guilt, judgement, fear and definite resistance.

When did not being contactable become a rarity? And we wonder why we feel tired a lot of the time.

Long gone are the days when children played out and parents hadn't a clue where they were, but knew they came home when hungry.

When we allow our children and loved ones the trust and space to work things out on their own, and with their own innate wisdom, they grow in their autonomy.

In not being an immediate contact for problem solving, or a witness for their happiness, they develop lifelong skills at managing their own emotional needs.

They grow up with more trust in themselves than they would if they are NOT given space to experience their own 'don't knows'.

Maybe that's it, maybe it's more about our own need to be needed, valued and reassured that all is OK, whether that's with children, with other family members or close friends.

Of course, for younger children it's different, but when our children are adults, and there is still this pattern, then it's worth seeing for whose benefit and whose detriment it is serving.

♡

Possible indicators and symptoms of being dependent on being contactable (amongst many more)

Rarely without phone, worrying that others will need you if you aren't contactable.

Soothing people's worries about your whereabouts or believing they have a need to know.

Wanting to know where loved ones are most of the time and feeling discomfort if you're not sure.

Excessively worrying about other people's safety as well as your own.

Relying on other people to be contactable for you to feel safe, settled and secure.

RECIPES FOR BEING UNCONTACTABLE

Recipe 1 – Gain or Detriment?

Recipe 2 – The Effects of Being Overly Available

Recipe 3 – Turning Your Phone Off

Recipe 1 – Gain or Detriment?

Make a list of what you gain from being contactable all or most of the time and make another list of things you miss out on or sacrifice when making yourself always openly available.

Sometimes we take our eye off the balance around this one and we hide behind feelings which being uncontactable brings up. In doing so, we can miss the detrimental effects which always being 'on call' can have on our nervous system.

Recipe 2 – The Effects of Being Overly Available

Take some time to truthfully look at the effects which always being contactable has on your mind, body (nervous system mainly) emotions and motivation.

Compare the above to how you feel when you've taken some time out.

Recipe 3 – Turning Your Phone Off

If you would like to proactively spend some time to compare how always being available feels against making time to not be, decide where it would be comfortable for you to start. It may be turning all phones off and having a cuppa in the garden, it may be a walk whilst leaving your phone at home, or it may be a weekend away.

You know what feels right for you and so start where you are now, not where you want to be.

This is about building trust and confidence back into your life around having time away from being there for loved ones. If you don't start from where you currently are, it may feel too much, and you won't start to build a wonderful opportunity in your life…to look forward to and LOVE time away from other people's requests of you.

For Your Notes...

CLOSING THOUGHTS

Reflections, resources, poems and recommendations that I value, and thought you may enjoy

LIFE'S SIMPLE RECIPES

Contents of Closing Thoughts

Epilogue 211
Afterword 214
Appendix: Maslow's Hierarchy of Needs 219
Appendix: Ancient Nahuati Blessing 220
What's Next? 222
Acknowledgements 225
Recommended Resources 230
Recommended Reading 232
Index of Recipes 234
About the Author 238
About Thoughtful Raven 240
A Reminder About Your Free Resources 241

LIFE'S SIMPLE RECIPES

CLOSING THOUGHTS

Epilogue

I hope that you have found some of these recipes a support for bringing more balance into your life, in a way which is simple and accessible.

The recipes in Part One anchor you when times are challenging and when you feel a little overwhelmed or anxious; Part Two dives a little deeper into knowing your continually evolving self, as and when time allows.

The great thing about recipe books is you can pick and mix for the occasion and this book is no different.

If you notice tiredness and restless sleep, you can look at those recipes. If you are sabotaging goals or holding resentments, you can look at those recipes.

Whatever your circumstances, I am sure there will be a recipe which will hold you still, for long enough to tip the scales back towards balance.

It's been a delight and a wonderful journey in writing this book and the recipes have held me through very emotional times.

They served me very well and I hope, with all my heart, that they can offer you the grounding they held for me, when needed the most.

I believe that when we look after and care for ourselves, it signals a safety for our energy to expand and open more.

Not only does expansion and opening our energy, nourish and replenish the life force in every cell and the DNA within our body, it gives space for the uncomfortable to stretch and become more spacious.

CLOSING THOUGHTS

The energy of our emotions and feelings were never designed to be held in a tight and closed environment.

If you are interested in courses, retreats or 1-1 work with me, information can be found at www.tiredandbusywomen.com.

I would love to hear your experiences of this book and welcome emails and shares.

Until then, I hope you continue to build the most beautiful and sacred relationship there is to build... the one with yourself, nothing excluded.

Much love,
Denice x

Afterword

Denice has written this book KNOWING that her recipes deliver beautiful results, because they are all born of walking her own talk.

This is the kind of book you can pick up and read once, or read it ten times, and you will get inspiration from it each and every time.

Whether it's one page, one recipe, or the whole book, you will find nuggets of wisdom and heaps of ideas that will make you think about your life – and more importantly, think about yourself. There are inspirations to help you find clarity, direction, even purpose amongst the busy-ness that occupies so much of life today.

Women are often wearing many different hats - as mothers, daughters, partners, lovers, carers, sisters, colleagues - and carry on regardless, stuffing everything inside at the expense of their own health and well-being - mentally, emotionally, spiritually, and physically - because life is so crowded. For all of these women, this book is like a personal therapist to have by your side at all times, to refer to, and find help.

A key point Denice makes is about creating space for stillness - even for just 30 seconds. Modern life can be noisy and crowded from the second you wake up, to the moment you go to bed, and then you wonder why you can't get to sleep. Full of your phone noise, visual noise, calls for your attention, mental distractions, questions, radio, TV, social media noise, listening to other people talking, environmental noise, and the noise of constantly rushing everywhere, from one thing to the next.

When you look at your daily life, it's very likely you are distracted in some way, perhaps most of the time. And it's not just distracted from being still, but being distracted from yourself too.

If there is no space for YOU in your day, you cannot create change.

Denice helps you to become very aware of where, and what, the distractions are, with her recipes gently guiding you to a place of stillness and silence and how to be comfortable in this space. And the deeper questions she asks you to consider in Part Two allow you to develop a true relationship with yourself – a concept which many women will put at the bottom of the 'to do' list. Yet, as Denice explains, knowing yourself and meeting your personal needs is the most important relationship of all.

Life's Simple Recipes is about introducing small, sensible, practical changes to then bring about much bigger change, rather than making dramatic all-encompassing changes, which often creates feelings of overwhelm and inertia.

Just as you would gather your ingredients, become familiar with them, then blend everything together

CLOSING THOUGHTS

to create something new and wonderful, so Denice has written her recipes to help you take that most important first step and be comfortable to continue creating change. Her recipes have very clear steps to follow which are succinctly and practically presented, to help you find the balance you are looking for.

I've known Denice for 18 years. We have walked a path of personal healing, well-being and exploring the bigger picture of life together, and I know she comes from a place of deep truth in writing this book. Her words are not empty words - they are words she lives herself, full of wisdom, full of love, and full of knowing that the ingredients, steps, principles and tools she offers you really do help, and really do make a difference.

For every woman, of every age, I invite you to share these recipes with other women you know. Teach your young ones the simple act of stopping, alongside the importance of stillness and the value of building a true relationship with yourself.

First and foremost, practice the recipes for yourself and notice the difference they start to make in your life.

Life's Simple Recipes for Bringing Tired and Busy Women into Balance will change your life.

Shelley Sishton
Author and Story Weaver,
Flower Medicine Teacher. Film Producer.
www.shelleysishton.com

Appendix:
Maslow's Hierarchy of Needs

As mentioned in Cleaning Your Kitchen at the beginning of Part One and see Free Resources at the back of the book.

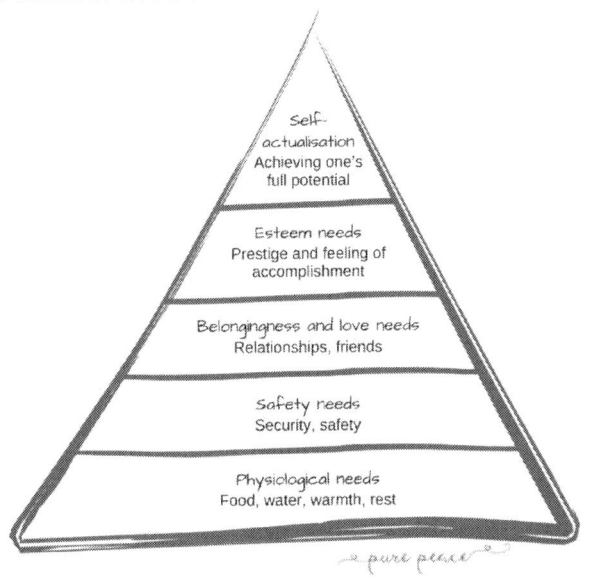

- Self-actualisation: Achieving one's full potential
- Esteem needs: Prestige and feeling of accomplishment
- Belongingness and love needs: Relationships, friends
- Safety needs: Security, safety
- Physiological needs: Food, water, warmth, rest

A Theory of Human Motivation. A. H. Maslow (1943). Originally Published in Psychological Review, 50, 370-396

Appendix: Ancient Nahuati Blessing

As mentioned in the chapter on Resentment and see Free Resources at the back of the book.

"I release my parents from the feeling that they have already failed me.

I release my children from the need to bring pride to me; that they write their own ways according to their hearts, that whisper all the time in their ears.

I release my partner from the obligation to complete myself. I do not lack anything; I learn with all beings all the time.

I thank my grandparents and forefathers who have gathered so that I can breathe life today.

I release them from past failures and unfulfilled desires, aware that they have done their best to resolve their situations within the consciousness that had at that moment.

CLOSING THOUGHTS

I honour you; I love you and I recognise you as innocent.

I am transparent before your eyes, so they know that I do not hide or owe anything other than being true to myself and to my very existence.

That walking with the wisdom of the heart, I am aware that I fulfil my life project, free from invisible and visible family loyalties that might disturb my Peace and Happiness, which are my only responsibilities.

I renounce the role of saviour, of being one who unites or fulfils the expectations of others.

Learning through, and only through LOVE, I bless my essence, my way of expressing, even though somebody may not understand me.

I understand myself, because I alone have lived and experienced my history; because I know myself, I know who I am, what I feel, what I do and why I do it. I respect and approve of myself. I honour the Divinity in me and in you...we are free."

What's Next?

If this book has inspired you to continue with expansion and balance, then I have some exciting news for you.

I am planning, and it may well exist by the time you are reading this, both a digital course and an online group course.

These courses will provide you with videos, worksheets, journal prompts and other resources for each chapter.

They will support you to spend more focused time with these themes and to integrate recipes to create a felt sense of balanced living. The courses will be well-structured, easy to follow and won't overwhelm.

CLOSING THOUGHTS

There will be regular Zoom calls so that you can bring conversations into a safe group setting and share with others.

I also offer 1-1 support to cover these recipes and to personalise where balance is most difficult for you. We work together to support the change and movement you want.

We start from where you are right now and we know that this 'where you are' changes all of the time. These calls are gentle, powerful and a loving support to have in your life. Not essential but most definitely valuable.

I create and deliver workshops, wellness walks, stillness events and retreats covering these themes.

I offer a low-cost monthly membership with fortnightly Zoom meetings, and a chance to have a cuppa and bring what's happening and what's real.

I run a free private Facebook Group called 'Supporting Tired & Busy Women Back To Balance' This is a group where you can ask questions, enjoy free resources and have a safe space to reflect and share within. I approve all members, so it may take a few days for you to be accepted as a member to the group.

My work is focused on supporting women to know what they need for their own sense of balance.

A feeling of dependency and need for anything I offer is strongly and verbally discouraged. Instead, we are looking towards you deepening trust in your own inner resources and become a strong advocate for yourself.

All of my offerings are to be found on www.tiredandbusywomen.com.

CLOSING THOUGHTS

Acknowledgements

So much gratitude I want to share with so many people, but I will start with my husband **Lewis**, for always encouraging me to take all the time I need in anything I want to spend time with.

For truly seeing and loving me unconditionally for so many years and in doing so, teach me to hold myself in that same love. He is my rock and I love him deeply.

Thanks to **Sam** and **Abi** for giving me the reason to want to be the best person I can be and for pulling me into the space of family life. This is the space in which I've learnt and grown the most in my life and being a Mum to you is an utter privilege and honour.

I couldn't be prouder as to who and how you are in this world. I love you unconditionally.

For all my teachers and friends, so many I could name but I am particularly grateful to:

Shelley Sishton, for guiding me into my energetic life, especially my health, for the wisest of conversations/teachings and for always reminding me not only of the sacredness of life but the beauty of my own.

I want to acknowledge Shelley for the time and love she put into reading my manuscript and for trusting our friendship enough to speak and share her feedback honestly and with such precision.

I am grateful for our friendship Shelley; I love you dearly and am excited for the adventures that you and I are still to share together in this world (and beyond).

Helena Skoog for sharing your heart with me in a way that allows us to be who we are when we are together; aligned, powerful and what a team we are! You are a precious friend; I love you dearly and am grateful for your presence in my life.

Sara Priestly for creating the **Birth Your Book Course**, without which THIS book would not be in your hand. Sara has offered incredible support, time, patience and guidance. She never once gave any opinions or ideas of content; instead, she was laser sharp in creating light conversation for my true content to naturally emerge.

I can't recommend this course enough, thank you Sara.

Diane Walker, who has consistently shaken her pom poms in encouragement for this book to be in your hand. Without her consistent question over the years, "When can I read your book Denice" I'm pretty sure this book wouldn't have arrived in the world at this time. Diane not only planted seeds for me to become a published writer, but she delicately watered and nurtured those seeds, and I am truly grateful, thank you.

My Dad, who encouraged me throughout my whole life, to be myself. He had an unwavering belief that I AM always enough and although it pained him to see I wasn't connecting with his words, he never stopped telling me.

It is only at the age of 51 (at the time of writing this book) that I fully understand the deeper wisdom within that love, and I thank him for seeing me.

My Dad was dying whilst I was writing. So this book became my research whilst navigating his death and the extreme stress which blew up in the aftermath.

I believe it was no coincidence that I was researching these recipes at such a time, and it truly allowed me to put them to the test. I was tired, I was exhausted physically, emotionally and spiritually, and these recipes did indeed bring me back to MY balance.

I miss you Dad and I am enjoying the new relationship we now have.

CLOSING THOUGHTS

And finally, I want to thank all my customers, clients and retreat/workshop participants, without whom, I would never have entered deeply into this work and discovered how much I am to share with the world.

And my biggest acknowledgment is to those who have this book and spent time with it.

I truly believe that if everyone made peace with all that they are and took radical responsibility for their life, we would indeed live with world peace, and this is my greatest vision and wish for us all.

Love, Peace and unapologetically YOU celebrations.

Denice x

Recommended Resources

You will also find a copy of these links in my Free Resources.

Your Free Resources:
bit.ly/tr_tired_busy_women
This is where you'll find the free resources I offer alongside this book!

Pure Peace:
www.pure-peace.co.uk
Candles & Natural Body Care Products to nourish yourself with, whilst you wrap yourself in the energy of love.

Tired & Busy Women:
www.tiredandbusywomen.com
Resources, events, workshops, retreats and 1-1 supported work with Denice Cartwright.

Shelley Sishton:
www.shelleysishton.com

Author and Story Weaver, Flower Medicine Teacher, Film Producer and an abundance of wisdom found here.

Forest Bathing:
www.forestbathingsussex.co.uk

Forest Bathing doesn't get more magical than with Helena - featured on Chelsea Flower Show 2024.

Sara Priestley:
www.sarapriestley.com

Sara Priestly offers not only the amazing Birth Your Book Course, but many other courses, workshops and memberships. I thoroughly recommend anything Sara shares if it holds resonance for you.

Marion Young:
www.marionyoung.co.uk

Marion Young's Conscious Resting is the most beautiful space to rest for a while within. For all things Stillness, Marion is an expert.

Recommended Reading
(to name just a few)

You will find a downloadable copy of this list in my online Free Resources (see the link at the back of the book).

Anatomy of the Spirit, Caroline Myss

Atlas of the Heart, Brene Brown

Celestine Prophecy, James Redfield

Doing Less, Kate Northrup

Dying To Be Me, Anita Moorjani

Heart Minded, Sarah Blondin

I May Be Wrong, Bjorn Natthiko Lindeblad

Mutant Message Down Under, Marlo Morgan

CLOSING THOUGHTS

Oneness With All Life, Eckhart Tolle

Practising The Power of Now, Eckhart Tolle

Quintessence: The Poetry of True Nature, Sara Priestley

Silence in the Age of Noise, Erling Kagge

The Body Keeps the Score, Bessel Van Der Kolk

The Complete Book of Awakening, Helen Amery & Sara Priestley

The Four Agreements, Don Miguel Ruiz

The Game of Life and How To Play It, Florence Scovel Shinn

The Magic Path of Intuition, Florence Scovel Shinn

The Man Who Planted Trees, Jean Giono

When The Body Says No, Gabor Mate

You Can Heal Your Life, Louise Hay

Index of Recipes

PART ONE 1

DEHYDRATION 7
   Recipe 1 – Cellular Hydrating Linseed Tea 12
   Recipe 2 – Staying Hydrated 13
   Recipe 3 – Put Hydration to the Test 14
   Recipe 4 – Making Hydration Easier 15
   Recipe 5 – Hydration Reminders 16

SLEEP & REST... 19
   Recipe 1 – Sleeping Environment 24
   Recipe 2 – Clearing the Mind.................................. 25
   Recipe 3 – Sleep Routines 26
   Recipe 4 – Move Towards Tired 27
   Recipe 5 – Conscious Resting 28

MESS & CLUTTER 31
   Recipe 1 – Feeling into Clutter 36
   Recipe 2 – Power Clear-Ups................................... 37
   Recipe 3 – Digital Tidy-Up 38
   Recipe 4 – Letting Go... 39

CLOSING THOUGHTS

SLOWING DOWN TO GET MORE DONE........................ *41*
   Recipe 1 – Stop, Pause & Slow Down 46
   Recipe 2 – Slowing Down 47
   Recipe 3 – One Thing at a Time 49
   Recipe 4 – Doing More in Less Time 50
   Recipe 5 – Powerful Mini Pauses 51

SELF-SABOTAGE *53*
   Recipe 1 – Hearing Self-Sabotage 58
   Recipe 2 – Do You Want It? 60
   Recipe 3 – There Is No Perfect Time 61

JUDGEMENT *65*
   Recipe 1 – Daily Check In 70
   Recipe 2 – Acknowledge What You Like About YOU . 72
   Recipe 3 – Noticing Criticism 73

RESENTMENT *77*
   Recipe 1 - Resentments 82
   Recipe 2 – Fears And Worries 84
   Recipe 3 – Pausing Within Emotions 85

COMMITMENT *87*
   Recipe 1 – Getting Clear 92
   Recipe 2 – Making a Plan 93
   Recipe 3 – Accountability 94
   Recipe 4 – Visual Support & Reminders 95
   Recipe 5 – Declaration of Commitment 96

PART TWO 99

NERVOUS SYSTEM CALLING 103
   Recipe 1 – Nervous System Soothers 110
   Recipe 2 – Nervous System Triggers 111
   Recipe 3 – Sandwich of Support 112

MORE BALANCE IN WHAT YOU LOVE 115
   Recipe 1 - What Do You Love? 120
   Recipe 2 – What One Thing? 121
   Recipe 3 – Reflection & Planning 122
   Recipe 4 – Knowing Our Neutralisers 123
   Recipe 5 – Habits, People Pleasing and Clarity 124
   Recipe 6 – Progress NOT Perfection 126

SAFETY 129
   Recipe 1 – Feeling Safe 134
   Recipe 2 – Feeling the Weight 136

KINDNESS AS A VALUE 139
   Recipe 1 - How Does Kindness Look for You? 144
   Recipe 2 – What Feels Unkind to You? 145
   Recipe 3 – Shifting Towards More Kindness 146
   Recipe 4 – How Do You Offer Yourself Kindness? .. 147
   Recipe 5 – Daily Acts of Kindness 148

CLOSING THOUGHTS

CLUTTERED THINKING, BELIEFS AND HABITS 153
   Recipe 1 – Journalling Emotional Themes 158
   Recipe 2 – Whose Responsibility Is This? 159
   Recipe 3 – Do They Know Who You Think They Are? 160
   Recipe 4 – People Pleasing Is to Please Ourselves. 161
   Recipe 5 – Moving On from Cluttered Thinking 162
   Recipe 6 – Subtle Expectations 163

LONELINESS 165
   Recipe 1 – Time Alone 170
   Recipe 2 – Asking Questions of Yourself 173
   Recipe 3 – What One Thing? 174
   Recipe 4 – A Date with YOU 175

BEING COMFORTABLE WITH QUIETNESS 177
   Recipe 1 – Making Time to Pause 182
   Recipe 2 – A Quiet Cuppa 184
   Recipe 3 – Turning Down the Noise 185

UNPLUGGING 187
   Recipe 1 – What You'd Like to Make Time For 192
   Recipe 2 – Plan Some Time to Unplug 193
   Recipe 3 – Enjoy Sharing Unplugged Time 194

BEING UNCONTACTABLE 197
   Recipe 1 – Gain or Detriment? 202
   Recipe 2 – The Effects of Being Overly Available 203
   Recipe 3 – Turning Your Phone Off 204

About the Author

My name is Denice, and I am thrilled to bring my passion of stillness and the art of creating balance, into the lives of women. Women who often feel tired, overwhelmed and who at times can feel deeply sensitive and often anxious.

I advocate for women to feel safe and heard, because women who feel safe and heard, grow and show more of their true selves to the world.

Women who feel safe and heard are more able to acknowledge and support themselves through their own vulnerabilities; so that they don't expect or put that role on to those in their lives.

Women who take radical responsibility for their own lives often grow to know themselves better, build a solid and truthful relationship with themselves, based on the foundation of compassion, non-judgement and deep love.

CLOSING THOUGHTS

I believe that once we hold ourselves in such a way, then and only then can we truly hold others within that very same unconditional energy. This for me, is what supports our life to be one of balance, one of happiness and one of freedom. This is what I LOVE to work with women on and it delights me to do so.

I guess I should share that I have over 33 years of working professionally with women. This has been in the fields of psychology, mental health, education, clinical practice, wellness, fostering & hypnotherapy, therapeutic counselling, play therapy, social work and life coaching.

I run wellness retreats, community wellness walks, women's circles, nervous system soothing workshops and I work 1-1 with women as a facilitator of balance and change. It's an utter joy and a privilege.

I am just a conversation a way...
Much love, Denice x

About Thoughtful Raven

Thoughtful Raven is a collaboration between Helen Amery and Sara Priestley (international Amazon best-sellers in spirituality). We offer a home for writers on topics on and around spirituality.

We help authors with the entire publishing process, offer promotion for books that fit our remit, and provide an opportunity to build supporting courses on an established platform.

You can find us at thoughtfulraven.co.uk

CLOSING THOUGHTS

A Reminder About Your Free Resources

bit.ly/tr_tired_and_busy_women

This is where you'll find the free resources I offer alongside this book. There are pdfs to download, audios, videos and links to get in touch with me. I look forward to our conversation.

Much love, Denice x

Printed in Great Britain
by Amazon